Pigs

First published in Great Britain in 1996 by
BROCKHAMPTON PRESS
20 Bloomsbury Street, London WC1B 3QA
a member of the Hodder Headline Group

This series of little gift books was made by Frances Banfield, Andrea P.A. Belloli, Polly Boyd,
Kate Brown, Stefano Carantino, Laurel Clark, Penny Clarke, Clive Collins, Jack Cooper, Melanie Cumming,
Nick Diggory, John Dunne, Deborah Gill, David Goodman, Paul Gregory, Douglas Hall, Lucinda Hawksley,
Maureen Hill, Dennis Hovell, Dicky Howett, Nick Hutchison, Douglas Ingram, Helen Johnson, C.M. Lee,
Simon London, Irene Lyford, John Maxwell, Patrick McCreeth, Morse Modaberi, Tara Neill, Sonya Newland,
Anne Newman, Grant Oliver, Ian Powling, Terry Price, Michelle Rogers, Mike Seabrook,
Nigel Soper, Karen Sullivan and Nick Wells.

ISBN 1 86019 4761
A copy of the CIP data is available from the British Library upon request.

Produced for Brockhampton Press by Flame Tree Publishing,
a part of The Foundry Creative Media Company Limited,
The Long House, Antrobus Road, Chiswick W4 5HY.

Printed and bound in Italy by L.E.G.O. Spa.

C E L E B R A T I O N

Pigs

Selected by Karen Sullivan

BROCKHAMPTON PRESS

On returning from a drive, the pig jumps about, making the most absurd antics to greet his friend the pony, and grunts a queer sharp grunt, looking for all the world like a fat and clumsy old spaniel greeting his master.

Letter to *The Spectator*, 1904

It is positively affecting to see how the sailors of HMS Glasgow in 1909 took a fancy to their ship's mascot, a large sow named Trotter.

Rev. J. G. Wood, *Petland Revisited*

A 28-year old American is trying to get the British interested in keeping pigs as pets. He says they are more intelligent than dogs and cleaner than cats. Mr Steve Zlotowitz has two 15-week-old pigs on sale for £10 each – but he cannot find the right buyer. He said: 'I don't like the way people are licking their lips when they look at them.'

Yorkshire Post

A pig that has two owners is sure to die of hunger.

Proverb

Toby, the Sapient Pig, The Only Scholar of his Race in the World, will Spell and Read, Cast Accounts, Play at Cards, Tell any Person what o'Clock it is to a Minute by Their Own Watch…

Handbill, 19th-century

If you would be happy for a week kill a pig; if you would be happy for a month take a wife; but if you would be happy all your life, plant a garden.

Proverb

The Naughty One
of the Family

Casting pearls before a swine.

Proverb

This little pig went to market;
This little pig stayed at home;
This little pig had roast beef;
This little pig had none;
And this little pig cried, 'Wee wee wee,
I can't find my way home!'

Nursery rhyme

Let's go to the wood, says this pig,
What to do there? says that pig,
To look for my mother, says this pig,
What to do with her? says that pig,
Kiss her to death, says this pig.

Gaelic rhyme

Home again, home again,
jiggedy jig.
My home is my castle
said Percy the pig.

Anonymous

7

No one has yet, so far as we are aware, adopted the pig as a drawing-room pet; and yet, if tended, there is no reason why he should not shine in that capacity. He would not run up the curtains like a kitten, nor knock down valuable ornaments from the chimney-piece...

G. A. Henty, *Those Other Animals*

Passer-by, contemplate here the mortal remains of the pig which acquired for itself imperishable glory by the discovery of the salt springs of Lunenburg.

Black marble memorial to a pig, Lunenburg, Hannover

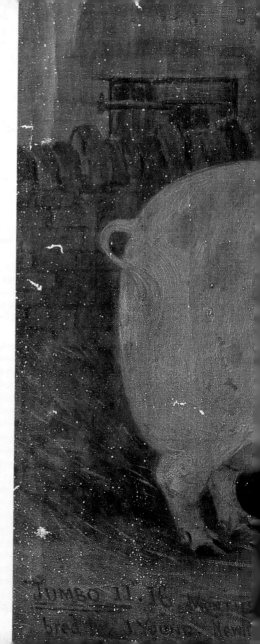

It was part of the Texas ritual.
We're rich as son-of-a-bitch stew
but look how homely we are, just
as plain-folksy as Grandpappy
back in 1836. We know about
champagne and caviar but we
talk hog and hominy.

Edna Ferber, *Giant*

Weight 41st 2lb
Fed by G BRANCH LEALHOLM

You'll find yourself in bed in something less than a pig's whisper.

Charles Dickens, *Pickwick Papers*

The Countess of Mount Edgcumbe erected an obelisk in memory of her pet pig, Cupid, at the end of the 18th century. Cupid was buried in a gold casket, having been the Countess's most faithful companion.

Old women are picking up twigs and acorns, and pigs of all sizes are doing their utmost to spare them the latter part of the trouble.

Mary Russell Mitford, *Our Village*

Tom, Tom, the piper's son,
Stole a pig, and away did run,
The pig was eat, and Tom was beat,
And Tom went howling down the street.

Nursery rhyme

There in a wood a Piggy-wig stood
With a ring at the end of his nose.

Edward Lear, *'The Owl and the Pussycat'*

'Dear Pig, are you willing to sell for one shilling
Your ring?' Said the Piggy, 'I will.'

Edward Lear, *'The Owl and the Pussycat'*

They roll and rumble,
They turn and tumble,
As pigges do in a poke.

Sir Thomas More, *Works*

'The time has come,' the Walrus said,
To talk to many things:
Of shoes – and ships – and sealing wax -
Of cabbages – and kings –
And why the sea is boiling hot –
And whether pigs have wings.'

Lewis Carroll, *'The Walrus and the Carpenter'*

'This magnificent animal,' continued the loud speaker, 'is truly terrific. Look at him ladies and gentlemen! Note the smoothness and whiteness of the coat, observe the spotless skin, the healthy pink glow of ears and snout... Note the general radiance of this animal!'

E. B. White, *Charlotte's Web*

America is no place for an artist: to be an artist is to be a moral leper, an economic misfit, a social liability. A corn-fed hog enjoys a better life than a creative writer, painter, or musician. To be a rabbit is better still.

Henry Miller

On a summer day when the heat brings thirst
A lion and a pig arrived at the same spring
And at once stared arguing
As to which of them should drink the water first.
They had such violent words
They would have fought to the death
Had they not noticed, in a pause for breath,
Vultures circling, waiting to feed
On which ever animal came off worst.
They made peace quickly. 'Better for us,' they agreed,
'To be friends than food for carrion birds.'

Aesop, *The Lion and the Pig*

An old lady was the owner of a small farm and prided herself on the neatness of everything, although she owned only a few animals. She was a bit concerned about her prize pig who had looked under the weather lately and thought that perhaps what she required was the attention of a male pig.

Passing the neighbouring farm on market day the old lady decided to call to ask if the farmer would allow his male pig to do the necessary. The farmer agreed and told her to bring her sow around the next day. Not owning any form of transport, the old lady decided to sit her pig in the wheelbarrow and push it to her neighbour's farm.

'Now just leave these two pigs alone for half an hour whilst we go in to have a cup of tea and I'm sure that the job will be done by the time we return. But if in another two days your pig seems as restless as before, bring her back and we'll give them the afternoon together.'

Two days passed and the pig again began to look restless, so out came the wheelbarrow and again the pig was pushed to the neighbouring farm.

The same instructions were given by the farmer, until by the end of the week tread marks were noticeable along the country land between the two farms.

'I'm sure that it must have taken by now,' thought the farmer, so he decided to give his neighbour a call.

'Does she still look listless?' he asked over the phone.

'I don't know,' said the old lady, 'because I can't see the field from here. Just hold the line while I nip upstairs and look through the bedroom window.'

A few minutes passed before the receiver was lifted again.

'Can you see her?' asked the farmer.

'Yes, yes,' he was told.

'And what is she doing?' he wanted to know.

'She's sat in the wheelbarrow,' said the old lady.

The Huge Joke Book

'Babe!' said Fly to the pig. 'That was quite beautifully done, dear.'

'Thank you so much!' said Babe to the sheep. 'You did that so nicely!'

'Ta!' said the sheep. 'Ta! Ta! Ta-a-a-a-a-a! 'Tis a pleasure to work for such a little gennulman!' And Ma added, 'You'll make a wunnerful sheep-pig, young un, or my name's not Ma-a-a-a-a.'

As for Farmer Hogget, he heard none of this, so wrapped up was he in his own thoughts. He's as good as a dog, he told himself excitedly, he's better than a dog, better than any dog! I wonder...!

'Good Pig,' he said.

Then he uncrossed his fingers and closed the gate.

Dick King-Smith, *The Sheep-Pig*

Five adolescent suckling pigs
fanned out alongside their sleeping mamma;
each daughter big as an alsatian dog,
her five petticoat-pink starch-skinned girls.

Penelope Shuttle, *Killiow Pigs*

The animal I really dig
Above all others is the pig.
Pigs are noble, Pigs are clever.
Pigs are courteous.

Roald Dahl, *The Three Little Pigs*

Pink pig
Black pig
Spotted pig
Sow
'Oh,' said the swineherd,
'I long for a cow.'

English rhyme

Pigs grow fat where lambs
would starve.

Proverb

'Tracks,' said Piglet. 'Paw-marks.'
He gave a little squeak of excitement.
'Oh, Pooh! Do you think it's a-a-a-a Woozle?'

A. A. Milne, *Winnie-the-Pooh*

Why did You make me so tender?
What a fate!
Lord,
teach me how to say
Amen.

Carmen Bernos de Gasztold, *The Prayer of the Little Pig*

Animals are in possession of themselves; their soul is in possession of their body. But they have no right to their life, because they do not will it.

Georg Hegel

'What pleasure,' said Aunt Dorcas feelingly – 'what possible pleasure can there be in entering a shop where you knock your head against a ham? A ham that may have belonged to a dear second cousin?'

Beatrix Potter, *The Tale of Little Pig Robinson*

'The pig,' quoth I, 'is burn'd.'

William Shakespeare, *The Comedy of Errors*

The sow ('sus' in Latin) is so called because it ploughs up its food; that is, it roots for food in the earth it has disturbed. The pig (porcus) is a filthy beast; it sucks up filth, wallows in mud, and smears itself with slime. Horace calls the sow 'the lover of mud'. Sows signify sinners, the unclean and heretics: it is prescribed in Jewish law that the flesh of beasts with cloven hooves which do not chew the cud shall not be eaten by the faithful. The Old and New Testaments, the Law and the Gospels, support this: because heretics do not chew the cud of spiritual food, they are unclean. Sows are those who neglect their penance and return to that which they once bewailed, as Peter says in his Epistle: The dog is turned to his own vomit again, and the sow that was washed to her wallowing in the mire.

An English Bestiary, 1220

The Pig: swine (swìn), cloven-hoofed mammals of the family Suidae, native to the Old World and typified by long, mobile snouts, thick, bristly hides, and small tails. Domesticated swine, commonly called hogs or pigs (the latter more correctly reserved for young swine), are probably descended chiefly from the wild swine, or wild boar *(Sus scrofa),* of Eurasia and N Africa.

Dictionary definition

The wind was against them now, and Piglet's ears streamed behind him like banners as he fought his way along.

A. A. Milne, *Winnie-the-Pooh*

Once I ran at a fair in the noise
To catch a greased piglet
That was faster and nimbler than a cat,
Its squeal was the rending of metal.

Ted Hughes, *'View of a Pig'*

In doing of either, let wit bear a stroke,
For buying or selling of pigs in a poke.

Thomas Tusser, *Five Hundred Points of Good Husbandry*

Knock, knock, knock.

'Who's there?' asked the pig, knowing full well what snarling, sharp-toothed devil of a wolf stood on the other side of his door.

'Tis only I, your friendly neighbour,' said the wolf with feeling.

'Oh, no it's not!' shouted the pig. 'It's the wolf!'

'Let me in,' said the wolf.

'Not by the hair of my chinny chin chin,' said the pig.

'Then I'll huff, and I'll puff and I'll blow the house in,' said the wolf.

And he did.

And he gobbled the pig up.

The Three Little Pigs

Let Grill be Grill and have his hoggish mind.

Edmund Spenser, *'The Fairie Queene'*

'D'you want a peppermint pig, Mrs Greengrass?'

Poll looked at him, thinking of sweets, but there was a real
pig poking its snout out of the milkman's coat pocket. It was
the tiniest pig she had ever seen. She touched its hard little
head and said, 'What's a peppermint pig?'

'Not worth much,' Mother said. 'Only a token. Like a
peppercorn rent. Almost nothing.'

Nina Bawden, *The Peppermint Pig*

It did so happen that persons had a single office divided
between them, who had never spoken to each other in their
lives, until they found themselves, they knew not how,
pigging together, heads and points, in the same truckle bed.

Edmund Burke, Speech on American taxation, 1774

40

41

So he went to work for
one of the citizens of that
country, who sent him out
to his farm to take care of
the pigs. He wished he
could fill himself with the
bean pods the pigs ate,
but no one gave him
anything to eat.

Luke, XV:16

The Empress of Blandings

Name of a pig in novels
by P. G. Wodehouse

Do not throw your pearls in front of pigs – they will
only trample them underfoot.

Matthew, VII:6

Not far away there was a large herd of pigs feeding.
So the demons begged Jesus, 'If you are going to drive
us out, send us into that herd of pigs.'

'Go,' Jesus told them; so they left and went off into
the pigs. The whole herd rushed down the side of the
cliff into the lake and was drowned.

Matthew, VIII:32

They wallowed like two porkers in a poke.

Geoffrey Chaucer, *'The Reeve's Tale'*

Besides 'tis known he could speak Greek,
As naturally as pigs squeak.

Samuel Butler, *Hudibras*

He had a cross of metal set with stones
And in a glass, a rubble of pig bones.
And with these relics, any time he found
Some poor up-country parson to astound.

Geoffrey Chaucer, *'The Prologue'*

Thou elvish-markt, abortive, rooting hog!

William Shakespeare, *Richard III*

Mother said, 'Give a pig a chance to keep clean and he'll take it, which is more than you can say of some humans. You tell me now, does Johnnie smell?'

If he did, it was only of a mixture of bran and sweet milk which was all he ate to begin with, although as he grew older, Mother boiled up small potatoes and added scraps from the table…'What he eats is important,' she said. 'Pigs are a poor person's investment.'

Nina Bawden, *The Peppermint Pig*

O monstrous beast – how like a swine he lies!

William Shakespeare, *The Taming of the Shrew*

They did not have to make beds for the hogs, because hogs
make their own beds and keep them clean.

Laura Ingalls Wilder, *Farmer Boy*

To market, to market, to buy a fat pig,
Home again, home again, jiggety-jig;
To market, to market, to buy a fat hog,
Home again, home again, jiggety-jog.

English nursery rhyme

 50

'I am going to fetch Lucy to eat up the rinds.'
'You will not do any such a thing!' Eliza Jane said. 'The idea!
A dirty old pig in the front yard!'
'She is not, either, a dirty old pig!' said Almanzo. 'Lucy's a little,
young, clean pig, and pigs are the cleanest animals there are!
You just ought to see the way Lucy keeps her bed clean, and turns
it and airs it and makes it up every day. Horses won't do that,
or cows, nor sheep, nor anything else.'

Laura Ingalls Wilder, *Farmer Boy*

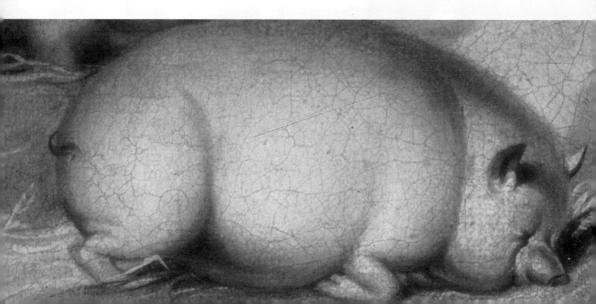

From the oyster to the eagle, from the swine to the tiger,
all animals are to be found in men and each of them exists in
some man, sometimes several at the time. Animals are
nothing but the portrayal of our virtues and vices made manifest
to our eyes, the visible reflections of our souls. God displays
them to us to give us food for thought.

Victor Hugo

'Where's Papa going with that axe?' said Fern to her mother as they were setting the table for breakfast.

'Out to the hoghouse,' replied Mrs Arable. 'Some pigs were born last night.'

'I don't see why he needs an axe,' continued Fern, who was only eight.

'Well,' said her mother, 'one of the pigs is a runt. It's very small and weak and it will never amount to anything. So your father has decided to do away with it.'

'Do *away* with it?' shrieked Fern. 'You mean *kill* it? Just because it's smaller than the others?'

E. B. White, *Charlotte's Web*

Watch out w'en you'er gittin all you want. Fattenin' hogs ain't in luck.

Joel Chandler Harris

Pigs are unclean and gluttonous men in the Gospel: 'If thou cast us out, suffer us to go away into the herd of swine' [*Matthew*, VIII:31]. And again: 'Neither cast ye your pearls before swine' [*Matthew*, VII:6]. The pig is also the man who is unclean of spirit: 'He sent him into his fields to feed swine' [*Luke*, XV:15]. The pig can signify both the unclean and the sinners, of whom it is written in the psalms: 'Their belly is filled with Thy hidden treasure: they are filled like swine, and leave what remains to their children' [*Luke*, XVII:14].

An English Bestiary, 1220

'By Jiminy, Grandpa,' shouted Jem. 'It's a pig. We are in the bacon!'

Miriam Frank, *The Farm*

One disadvantage of being a hog is that at any moment some
blundering fool may try to make a silk purse out of your wife's ear.

Beachcomber, *'By The Way'*

Piggy Sneed had absorbed, by the uniqueness of his retardation
and by his proximity to his animal friends, certain pig-like
expressions and gestures.

John Irving, *Trying to Save Piggy Sneed*

Odd things animals… only a pig looks at you as an equal.

Winston Churchill

The pig, if I am not mistaken,
Supplies us sausage, ham and bacon.
Let others say his heart is big –
I call it stupid of the pig.

Ogden Nash, *Happy Days*

I'm very fond of pigs, but I don't find it difficult to eat them.

Robert Runcie, Archbishop of Canterbury

Barber, barber, shave a pig,
How many hairs to make a wig?
Four and twenty, that's enough.
Give the barber a pinch of snuff.

English nursery rhyme

This pig got in the barn,
This ate all the corn,
This said he wasn't well,
This said he would go and tell,
And this said… weeke, weeke, weeke,
Can't get over the barn door sill.

English nursery rhyme

Where are you going, you little pig?
I'm leaving my mother, I'm growing so big!
So big, young pig!
So young, so big!
What leaving your mother, you foolish young pig?

Thomas Hood, *Little Piggy*

Friend of the fatherless!
Fountain of happiness!
Lord of the swill-bucket! Oh, how my soul is on
Fire when I gaze at thy
Calm and commanding eye,
Like the sun in the sky,
Comrade Napoleon!

Thou art the giver of
All that thy creatures love,
Full belly twice a day, clean straw to roll upon;
Every beast great or small
Sleeps at peace in his stall,
Thou watchest over all,
Comrade Napoleon!

Had I a sucking-pig,
Ere he had grown as big
Even as a pint bottle or a rolling-pin,
He should have learned to be
Faithful and true to thee,
Yes, his first squeak should be
'Comrade Napoleon!'

George Orwell, *Animal Farm*

This little pig went to market

Upon a cock-horse to market I'll trot,
To buy a pig to boil in the pot.
A shilling a quarter, a crown a side.
If it had not been killed, it would surely have died.

Anonymous

Jacob! I do not like to see thy nose
Turn'd up in scornful curve at yonder Pig.
It would be well, my friend, if we, like him,
Were perfect in our kind!... And why despise
The sow-born grunter?... He is obstinate,
Thou answerest; ugly, and the filthiest beast
That banquets upon offal... Now I pray you
Hear the Pig's Counsel...

Robert Southey, *The Pig*

Grandfa' Grig
Had a pig,
In a field of clover;
Piggy died,
Grandfa' cried,
And all the fun was over.

Traditional nursery rhyme

There was a lady loved a swine
Honey, quoth she,
Pig-hog wilt thou be mine?
Hoogh, quoth he.

Anonymous

Midnight sounded. The Bronze Pig stirred, and he heard
it say distinctly: 'Ho, little boy, hold fast; I'm off!'
And off it went on its magic ride!

Hans Andersen, *'The Bronze Pig'*

This making of Christians will raise the price of hogs.

William Shakespeare, *The Merchant of Venice*

Animals are such agreeable friends – they ask no questions,
they pass no criticisms.

George Eliot, *Scenes of Clerical Life*

What can you expect from a pig but a grunt?

Proverb

Whose little pigs are these, these, these?
Whose little pigs are these?
They are Roger the Cook's
I know by their looks;
I found them among my peas.
Go pound them, go pound them.
I dare not on my life,
For though I love not Roger the Cook
I dearly love his wife.

English country song

I think I could turn and live with animals, they
are so placid and self-contain'd,
I stand and look at them long and long.
They do not sweat and whine about their condition,
They do not lie awake in the dark and weep for their sins,
They do not make me sick discussing their duty to God,
Not one is dissatisfied, not one is demented
with the mania of owning things,
Not one kneels to another, nor to his kind that
lived thousands of years ago,
Not one is respectable or unhappy over the whole earth.

Walt Whitman, *'Leaves of Grass'*

Being a Georgia author is a rather specious dignity, of the same
order as, for the pig, being a Talmadge ham.

Flannery O'Connor

I have often remarked that the Devonshire farms have very strange names. If you had ever seen Piggery Porcombe you would think that the people who lived there were very queer too! Aunt Dorcas was a stout speckled pig who kept hens. Aunt Porcas was a large smiling black pig who took in washing. We shall not hear very much about them in this story. They led prosperous, uneventful lives and their end was bacon. But their nephew Robinson had the most peculiar adventures that ever happened to a pig.

Beatrix Potter, *Little Pig Robinson*

As a jewel of gold in a swine's snout, so is a fair woman which is without discretion.

Proverbs, XI:22

 74

'Presents,' I often say, 'endear absents.'

Charles Lamb, *'A Dissertation Upon Roast Pig'*

What men call social virtues, good fellowship,
is commonly but the virtue of pigs in a litter, which lie
close together to keep each other warm.

Henry David Thoreau

I have eyes like those of a dead pig.

Marlon Brando

Edible. Good to eat and wholesome to digest, as a worm to a toad,
a toad to a snake, a snake to a pig, a pig to a man,
and a man to a worm.

Ambrose Bierce, *The Devil's Dictionary*

There is no such thing as a perfect leader either in the past or
present, in China or elsewhere. If there is one, he is only
pretending, like a pig inserting scallions into its nose in an
effort to look like an elephant.

Liu Shao-ch'i

A hog on trust grunts till he's paid.

Proverb

Douglas Hall

A peasant becomes fond of his pig and is
glad to salt away its pork. What is significant,
and is so difficult for the urban stranger to
understand, is that the two statements are
connected by an and and not by a but.

John Berger

Some men there are love not a gaping pig,
Some that are mad if they behold a cat,
And others when the bag-pipe sings i'th nose
Cannot contain their urine.

William Shakespeare, *The Merchant of Venice*

'W-w-what medicine,' said Piglet.
'To make you grow big and strong, dear. You don't want to grow up
small and weak like Piglet, do you? Well then!

A. A. Milne, *Winnie-the-Pooh*

To buy a pig in a poke.

Proverb

He who cannot eat horsemeat need not do so. Let him eat pork.
But he who cannot eat pork, let him eat horsemeat.
It's simply a question of taste.

Nikita Khrushchev

Ireland is the old sow that eats her farrow.

James Joyce

A pretty pig makes an ugly sow.

Proverb

Notes on Illustrations

Page 1 *Three Prize Pigs Outside a Sty* by The English School, (Nineteenth Century) (Iona Antiques, London). Courtesy of The Bridgeman Art Library; **Page 3** *The Naughty One of the Family.* Courtesy of The Laurel Clark Collection; **Page 4** *Leaping Pig* by Douglas Hall; **Page 6** *The Gloucester Old Spot Pig Painted at Great Haywood Staffordshire.* Courtesy of the Bridgeman Art Library; **Page 8** *Over the Garden Fence* by Pat Scott (Private Collection). Courtesy of the Bridgeman Art Library; **Page 11** *The Prize Pig Jumbo 11* by W. S. P. Henderson (Bonhams, London). Courtesy of The Bridgeman Art Library; **Page 12** *Pigging Out* by Pat Scott (Private Collection). Courtesy of The Bridgeman Art Library; **Page 15** *Grunter Weekly* by Douglas Hall; **Page 17** *Pigs at a Trough* by George Morland (Maidstone Museum and Art Gallery, Kent). Courtesy of The Bridgeman Art Library; **Page 18** *A to D from 'An Alphabet of Old Friends'* by Walter Crane (Antony Crane Collection). Courtesy of The Bridgeman Art Library; **Page 21** *A Pig in its Sty* by E. M. Fox (Bonhams, London). Courtesy of The Bridgeman Art Library; **Page 24** *Mr and Mrs Pig and Family* by Douglas Hall; **Page 27** *'This Remarkable Animal...',* engraved by John Whessel by Benjamin Gale (Private Collection). Courtesy of the Bridgeman Art Library; **Page 28** *Confrontation* by The English School (Nineteenth Century) (Bonhams, London). Courtesy of The Bridgeman Art Library; **Page 30** *The Cat and the Fiddle and The Cow – Illustrations from Hey Diddle Diddle* by Randolph Caldecott (Private Collection). Courtesy of The Bridgeman Art Library; **Page 32** *Three Pigs with Castle in the Background* by The English School, (Nineteenth Century) (Iona Antiques, London). Courtesy of The Bridgeman Art Library; **Page 37** *Contemplating Pig in Public House* by Douglas Hall; **Page 38** *Two Prize Pigs in an Interior* by John Rathbone Harvey (Bonhams, London). Courtesy of The Bridgeman Art Library; **Page 41** *Neighbours.* Courtesy of The Laurel Clark Collection; **Page 42** *A Leicester Sow, Two Years Old, the Property of Samuel Wiley* by William Henry Davis (Private Collection). Courtesy of The Bridgeman Art Library; **Page 45** *Young Shavers.* Courtesy of The Laurel Clark Collection; **Page 47** *Three Prize Pigs Outside a Sty* by The English School, (Nineteenth Century) (Iona Antiques, London). Courtesy of The Bridgeman Art Library; **Page 48** *Pigging Out* by Pat Scott (Private Collection). Courtesy of The Bridgeman Art Library; **Page 51** *Dancing Pigs* by Douglas Hall; **Pages 52-3** *Three Pigs with Castle in the Background* by The English School (Iona Antiques, London). Courtesy of The Bridgeman Art Library; **Page 57** *He's No More Manners Than a Pig.* Courtesy of The Laurel Clark Collection; **Page 58** *A Field Day* by Pat Scott (Private Collection). Courtesy of The Bridgeman Art Library; **Page 61** *The Ultimate British Pig* by Derold Page (Private Collection). Courtesy of The Bridgeman Art Library; **Page 64** *This Little Pig Went to Market* Anonymous (Private Collection). Courtesy of The Bridgeman Art Library;

Page 66 *Pigs in a Sty* by James Ward (Rafael Valls Gallery, London). Courtesy of The Bridgeman Art Gallery; **Page 68** *Leap Frogging Pigs* by Douglas Hall; **Page 71** *Cottage Hospitality* by William Collins (Haworth Art Gallery, Accrington, Lancashire). Courtesy of The Bridgeman Art Library; **Page 72** *Farmyard Friends* by William Weekes (Hayes Fine Art at the Bindery Galleries). Courtesy of The Bridgeman Art Library; **Page 77** *Pavarotti Pigs* by Douglas Hall; **Page 78** *Pig in the String Section* by Douglas Hall; **Page 80** *A Field Day* by Pat Scott (Private Collection). Courtesy of The Bridgeman Library; **Pages 82-3** *Leap Frogging Pigs* by Douglas Hall.

Acknowledgements: The Publishers wish to thank everyone who gave permission to reproduce the quotes in this book. Every effort has been made to contact the copyright holders, but in the event that an oversight has occurred, the publishers would be delighted to rectify any omissions in future editions of this book. *Winnie-the-Pooh* and other titles, A.A. Milne, reprinted courtesy of Curtis Brown, Methuen Children's Books and E. P. Dutton, copyright renewed; *An English Bestiary* from the Bodleian Library, Oxford, MS Bodley 764; *The Peppermint Pig* © Nina Bawden, 1975, reprinted courtesy of Victor Gollancz Limited; *The Sheep-Pig* © Dick King-Smith, 1983, reprinted courtesy of Victor Gollancz Limited; Ted Hughes, from *Moon Bells and Other Poems,* Chatto & Windus, 1970, reprinted courtesy of Faber & Faber Ltd; extracts by Roald Dahl © Roald Dahl, reprinted courtesy of Unwin Hyman Limited, Jonathan Cape Limited and Penguin Books Limited; *Farmer Boy* copyright © Laura Ingalls Wilder, 1932, reprinted courtesy of Methuen Children's Books; Ogden Nash, from *Verses from 1929 on* reprinted by permission of Curtis Brown, Ltd. Copyright © 1942 by Ogden Nash, renewed; *The Huge Joke Book,* reprinted courtesy of Random House; *Charlotte's Web* copyright © E. B. White, 1952, reprinted courtesy of Hamish Hamilton Children's Books and Harper & Row Publishers Inc.; *The Tale of Little Pig Robinson,* Beatrix Potter, reprinted courtesy of Frederick Warne, a division of Penguin Book © Frederick Warne, renewed; Carmen Bernos de Gasztold, from 'The Prayer of the Little Pig' from *Prayers from the Ark,* translated by Rumer Godden, reprinted courtesy of Macmillan Publishing Company Ltd; Penelope Shuttle, from *Killiow Pigs,* reprinted courtesy of Oxford University Press; *Good News Study Bible,* published by Thomas Nelson, 1986, extracts reprinted with their kind permission; *Penguin Book of Japanese Verse,* translated by Geoffrey Bownas and Anthony Thwaite, published by Penguin 1964, and